Science Warriors

THE BATTLE AGAINST INVASIVE SPECIES

Written by Sneed B. Collard III

Houghton Mifflin Company Boston 2008

For my brother Dennis,
who always fights the good fight.

Many, many people contributed to making this book a reality. To all of you, I offer my heartfelt thanks not only for your help, but for the important work you do combating invasive species:

Brown Tree Snake Sections

Mike Pitzler and Daniel Vice, USDA-APHIS in Hawaii, Guam, and the Pacific Islands

Christopher Powell, 36th Wing Public Affairs, Andersen Air Force Base, Guam

Red Fire Ant Sections

At the Brackenridge Field Laboratory, University of Texas, Austin: Laurence Gilbert, Edward LeBrun, Kirsti Krejs, Jonathan Sprague, Ahmar Hashmi, Tonja Simons, Steven Gibson, Britt Dean, Joy Hernandez, and Angie Kaufman

Sanford Porter, USDA-ARS, Gainesville, Florida

John Longino, The Evergreen State College, Olympia, Washington

Melaleuca Sections

At USDA-ARS, Fort Lauderdale, Florida: Cressida Silvers, Ted Center, Paul Pratt, Min Rayamajhi, and John Scoles

Jim Creber, Applied Aquatic Management, Eagle Lake, Florida

Linda Rojas, Rojas Brothers Grove Service, Groveland, Florida

Zebra Mussel Sections

Douglas A. Jensen, University of Minnesota Sea Grant Program, Duluth

Allen Mesinger and Jean Stevenson, University of Minnesota, Duluth

Heidi Wolf, Minnesota Department of Natural Resources, St. Paul

Joe Starinchak, U.S. Fish and Wildlife Services, Arlington, Virginia

Philip Moy, University of Wisconsin Sea Grant Institute, Manitowoc

Angela Archer, Illinois-Indiana Sea Grant, Purdue University, West Lafayette, Indiana

I would also like to thank Lisa Diercks for turning this book into a work of art. Last—and foremost—a special cheer to my editor, Erica Zappy, for investing this project with limitless enthusiasm and skill. Thank you!

—Sneed B. Collard III

Photography Credits
Lawrence Gilbert: 12 (right)
Minnesota Department of Natural Resources: 46
Lisa K. Nordquist: 43
Airman First Class Daniel Owen, courtesy of Andersen Air Force Base: 4 (bottom)
Sanford Porter, USDA-ARS: 8, 10, 15, 16 (top right), 17, 21 (right)
United States Department of Agriculture: 44 (top)
United States Fish and Wildlife Service: 41 (bottom)
Daniel S. Vice, USDA/APHIS: 3, 4 (top), 7 (all images), 36 (all images), 37 (right)

All other photographs by Sneed B. Collard III

Maps by Jerry Malone

For information about permission to reproduce selections from this book, write to Permissions, Houghton Mifflin Company, 215 Park Avenue South, New York, New York 10003.
www.houghtonmifflinbooks.com

Library of Congress Cataloging-in-Publication Data is on file.

ISBN-13: 978-0-618-75636-0

Book design by Lisa Diercks
The text of this book is set in Avenir.

Manufactured in China
WKT 10 9 8 7 6 5 4 3 2 1

CHAPTER ONE:

Enemy at the Gates

On the U.S. island of Guam, Andersen Air Force Base is under siege. Nighttime patrols walk the fence line around the base, looking for any signs of intruders. Live traps are set every sixty to seventy-five feet along the perimeter. Inside the base, federal agents work with highly trained Jack Russell terriers, which sniff a load of equipment bound for Hawaii. This isn't a drill. The threat is real, and if security efforts fail, the Hawaiian Islands could become a disaster zone.

Under the watchful eye of her handler, one terrier walks toward a large military truck. The dog's sensitive nose filters the air for the tiniest odors. Suddenly, the hair on her neck stiffens and she sits down.

The agent steps forward, his heart racing. "Find it," he tells the terrier. Sniffing vigorously, the dog makes her way to the front of the truck and holds her paw out toward the engine compartment.

"Good girl," the handler tells her, slipping her a treat. After tying the dog's leash to a nearby crate, the agent turns on his flashlight and gets down on his knees to look under the truck's front end. Nothing. He carefully pops open the hood and scans the engine with the flashlight. Again, he doesn't see anything. Then, his flashlight beam freezes. Wrapped around the truck's master brake cylinder sits the stowaway—a three-foot-long brown tree snake.

Working quickly, the agent unwraps the struggling serpent from the brake cylinder. After placing the hissing reptile into a bag, the agent's heartbeat begins to return to normal and relief washes through him. It's one more close call. One more disaster narrowly averted.

ABOVE: Brown tree snakes are nocturnal and rarely seen during the day, but that doesn't keep them from having a big impact on Guam.

TOP LEFT:
Inspector-dog teams provide a last line of defense for keeping brown tree snakes out of critical cargo areas.

BOTTOM LEFT:
The high traffic of Andersen Air Force Base makes it a key facility for preventing the spread of brown tree snakes.

FACING PAGE:
Tamarisk trees are one of hundreds of plants that harm native ecosystems. Originally from Asia and the Mediterranean, the trees are sucking streams and rivers dry throughout the American West.

TERRESTRIAL TERROR

If the scene above sounds like it's from a war on terror, that's because in many ways, it is. But in this case, our enemies are not people. They are other kinds of organisms. Scientists call them *invasive species*.

What exactly are they?

Invasive species include a huge array of animals, plants, fungi, and diseases. They can be as large as a burro or too small to see with a microscope. Some are pleasing to look at; others hideous. But all invasive species have two things in common. First, they are "exotic" or "alien," meaning they are living somewhere they don't belong. Second, they are causing major problems in their new homes.

Invasive species are a global problem. In the United States alone, at least 6,200—and probably thousands more—alien, or exotic, species have become established from other parts of the world. They include insects, ornamental flowers, reptiles, trees, fungi, birds, viruses, mammals, bacteria—almost every kind of organism you can think of. Not all of these exotic species are considered invasive. Many are useful to people as food, pets, or simple entertainment, and most fit in pretty well once they are here. They may cause some minor problems, but most people hardly notice them.

Other exotic arrivals wreak havoc.

DIRTY DEEDS

Invasive species take a terrible toll on our economy, environment, and health. Weeds such as spotted knapweed and star thistle have choked

millions of acres of rangelands across the western United States, robbing cattle and wildlife of food and costing farmers billions of dollars to control. Alien birds such as the European starling devour millions of dollars' worth of crops each year and have driven some native birds toward extinction by taking over their nests. Exotic beetles have killed vast forests across our nation, while alien viruses have caused untold human misery in the form of AIDS, West Nile virus, and the flu. According to one scientific study, invasive species cost Americans approximately $137 *billion* each year. That's more than twice what the U.S. government spent on education in 2007.

The brown tree snake provides a vivid example of just how harmful an invasive species can be. Originally from Australia and nearby islands, the snake hitchhiked to the U.S. island of Guam shortly after World War II. In Guam, it found a new home free of predators and full of food. By the 1980s, more than 13,000 brown tree snakes filled every square mile of Guam. The serpents wiped out at least nine of Guam's native bird species, along with native geckos and most other vertebrates. The snakes began causing thousands of blackouts as they crawled across power lines. They literally devoured Guam's poultry industry. Even more alarming, they began biting people of all ages, sending many to hospital emergency rooms.

In one prolonged punch, this single species devastated Guam's environment, damaged its economy, and reduced the quality of life for the people who lived there. Yet the brown tree snake is only one of thousands of examples of invasive species that have had a negative impact on our nation and our planet. According to a report by the Office of Technology Assessment, by 1993 more than two hundred alien species in the United States had been classified as invasive. Today, scientists estimate that number is about 7,000. Scientists, in fact, consider the problem of invasive species to be one of the most urgent crises humans face on earth.

Scientists are also on the front lines, using every tool that they have to fight these harmful invaders.

ABOVE: Introduced from Europe, starlings now live in every one of the fifty states. In flocks of up to a million birds, they devour crops and rob native birds of nesting sites.

LEFT: In California alone, yellow star thistle has invaded more than 15 million acres. The plant dries out soils, and its thorny spines render grazing lands useless.

Brown tree snakes (LEFT) have devastated Guam's environment and seriously harmed its economy.

The white tern (RIGHT) is now extremely rare on Guam.

The bridled white-eye (BELOW RIGHT) and oceanic snake-eyed skink (BELOW LEFT) are just two Guam species that the brown tree snake drove to extinction.

CHAPTER TWO:

Fire in the Hole

In the heart of the Texas capital of Austin lies a tapestry of native woodlands and grasslands known as the Brackenridge Field Laboratory. The University of Texas runs the laboratory, and since 1980, biologist Larry Gilbert has been its director.

Larry is a Texas native to his core. His dad was a Presbyterian minister and a chaplain in the navy and in the Texas prison system. Every year or two, Larry's father took a job in a new place and his family moved along with him. Seeing the different parts of Texas made Larry appreciate his state's remarkable animals and plants. "I always went hunting and fishing with my grandfather and my uncle," he recalls. "I think all kids are interested in bugs, and I remember at about the age of nine or ten raising my first caterpillar. In the case of my parents, their view of the world was that it is the handiwork of God, so I had a free rein to study that."

It's no surprise that after finishing high school, Larry studied biology. He earned his Ph.D., or doctorate degree, by investigating the relationships between butterflies and plants. When he arrived at Brackenridge, he still focused on butterflies but was also impressed by the number of native ant species at the laboratory. "When I took over this place," he explains, "one of the things I was touting was

Millions of Americans know firsthand the burning sting of one of our nation's worst invaders, the red imported fire ant.

ABOVE: The invasion of Brackenridge Field Laboratory got Larry Gilbert thinking seriously about fire ants.

RIGHT: Larry Gilbert examines a fire ant mound at Brackenridge.

the fifty-five or so native ant species here. We had army ants, leaf-cutter ants, native fire ants—you know, all these different weird ants."

Then, only a year later, the red imported fire ant *Solenopsis invicta* arrived.

Within four or five years, the new invader completely dominated Brackenridge. It wiped out the laboratory's native ants, as well as a host of other species. There were so many fire ants that their mounds seemed

Fire ant workers fiercely defend eggs laid by their queens and will move them in response to threats or a change in temperature.

to cover every square yard of the laboratory's eighty-two acres. The swiftness and pattern of the invasion astounded Larry. But it would also lead him on a new research path—and into the jaws of the fire ant threat.

THE RED TIDE

No one is exactly sure when the red imported fire ant first arrived in the United States, but best guesses are in the late 1920s or early 1930s. Despite the name "red *imported* fire ant," the ant was not brought to our shores on purpose. Like an earlier invader, the black imported fire ant, it traveled from South America in rocks or dirt used as ballast in ships. This ballast was dumped at the port of Mobile, Alabama—along with its insect stowaways.

The fire ant liked its new home. In the southern United States, it found a comfortable climate free from parasites, predators, and other enemies it had faced in South America. Even better, humans helped it expand its range. Hitchhiking in grass sod, potted nursery plants, and other freight, the ant quickly rolled across the countryside. By 1953, the "red menace" had firmly infested ten southern states.

Wherever it landed, it transformed the local landscape. Living in colonies of up to a quarter million members, the red imported fire ant overwhelmed native ant populations, including the native fire ants that already lived here. The fire ant also devoured most other arthropods—hard-shelled animals such as spiders, scorpions, centipedes, and insects. Fire ants preyed on small birds, mammals, and reptiles. They did eat some crop pests, but they destroyed other crops, such as pecans. Their hard mounds damaged mowers, hay balers, and other farm equipment. Whenever they encountered human skin, the ants inflicted sizzling, painful stings that for some people caused serious injury and even death.

By the late 1950s, humans had had enough. We declared war with a massive poisoning program (see sidebar: "War Is Hell—Unless You're a Fire Ant"). We badly underestimated our enemy. The fire ant not only

ABOVE: The transport of sod and nursery plants greatly accelerated the spread of the red imported fire ant.

RIGHT: Caterpillars and other invertebrates don't stand a chance against marauding armies of red imported fire ants.

survived our offensive but emerged stronger than ever. By 2004, the red fire ant had infested 320 *million* acres in thirteen states—one-seventh of our nation's land area. It ranged from Florida to California and as far north as Tennessee. And in Larry Gilbert's home state of Texas, the ant unleashed its most potent weapon of mass destruction.

THE GENERAL PATTON OF ANTS

When *Solenopsis invicta* finally reached Brackenridge Field Laboratory, it wasn't just the scale of the invasion that impressed Larry Gilbert. It was the way it happened. "When we saw the pattern of invasion, that was just mind-boggling," Larry explains. "You tend to think of an ant invasion as a metastasizing cancer, where the winged queens rain down randomly, and each queen struggles to compete with native ants to start a new colony."

This invasion wasn't like that. "Instead," Larry describes, "it was more like Patton's tank invasion of Europe during World War II. On one side, you had the native ant communities—on the other side, the fire ants rolling over them. When I saw that pattern of spread, I was fascinated."

Larry decided to ask two of his postdoctoral colleagues to figure out why the fire ant invasion was so effective. What these researchers found was that the red fire ant colonies in Texas reproduced differently than most other red fire ants in the southeastern United States. Instead of one queen, they had evolved to have *many* queens.

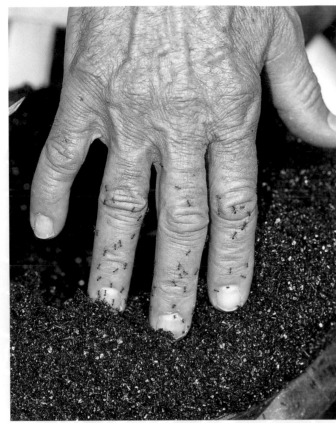

CLOCKWISE FROM UPPER LEFT:

Any disturbance of an ant mound sends fire ants boiling over their intruder, but before stinging, the ants need to firmly grasp a person's skin.

The size and number of fire ant mounds can easily damage farm equipment and have an impact on crop yields.

Fire ants come in many different sizes depending on their function within the colony.

THE POLYGYNE BOMB

Most ant colonies begin when another colony produces a crop of winged females that leave, or disperse. These "queen" ants mate with males in the air, then land and shed their wings to begin brand-new colonies. The new colonies are each separate units and are called monogyne (MAW-noh-jine), or "single queen," colonies. They compete for food and space with other colonies, even of their own species. "The monogyne queens probably live six to seven years," explains Dr. Ed LeBrun, a scientist who works with Larry. "And that will be the life span of a colony."

The red fire ants in Texas, however, do something different. They are polygyne (PAWL-ee-jine). They have evolved to have multiple queens. Neighboring ant mounds do not compete with or attack each other. Instead, they all thrive together, behaving as one giant insect organism.

Polygyne colonies can exist at *ten times* the densities of monogyne colonies. According to one researcher, they form "a kind of sheet of fire ants through the earth." They also never die out. When one queen dies, there are many others to replace her. As a result, they become a devastating force to reckon with.

Larry's observation of the fire ant invasions at Bracken-ridge and elsewhere in Texas convinced him that the poly-gyne fire ants formed a major threat to the Texas environment. The ant's impact on the state's economy was also becoming clear (see sidebar: "How Expensive Is an Ant?"). At the same time, Larry knew that poisoning the ants was never going to make more than a temporary dent in their popula-tions. Because of this, he and his colleagues began thinking of other ways to tame the red imported fire ant. Larry was especially interested in finding a biological control agent—another organism such as a disease, parasite, or predator that could control the fire ant. He and his team turned their attention to a group of poorly known flies called phorids.

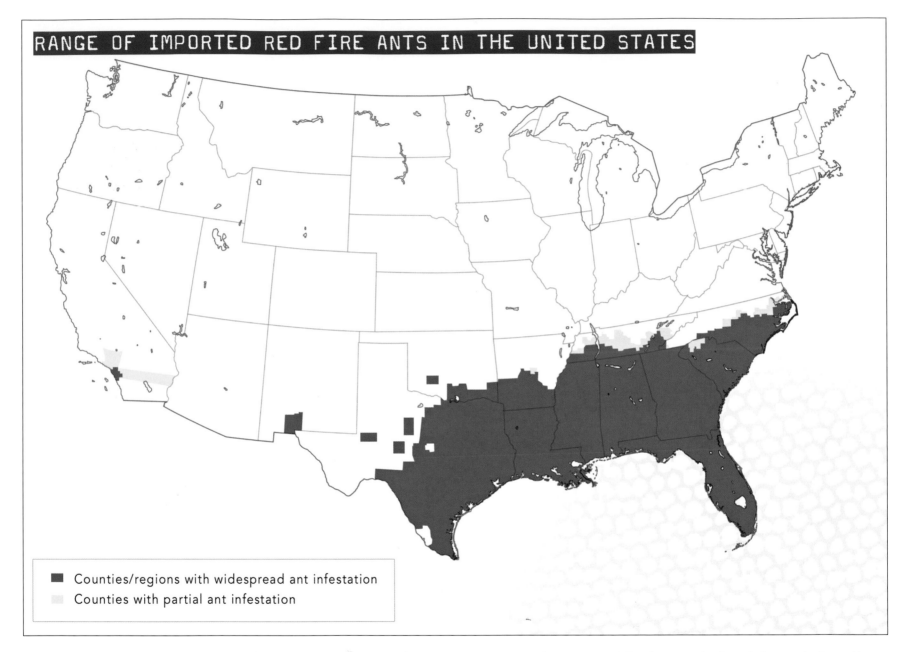

RANGE OF IMPORTED RED FIRE ANTS IN THE UNITED STATES

■ Counties/regions with widespread ant infestation
□ Counties with partial ant infestation

So far, the red imported fire ant has invaded all or part of thirteen states. Quarantines prevent the transport of certain goods from the affected areas in an effort to slow the ant's spread.

TINY TERRORS

Phorid (FORE-id) flies are tiny insects that parasitize ants. A female fly zooms in and inserts an egg directly into the body of an ant. The fly egg hatches into a larva that grows inside the ant, feeding on its tissues. Eventually, the larva kills the ant, forms a pupa, or cocoon, and hatches out into an adult fly.

Larry Gilbert first started thinking about phorid flies several years before the fire ant invasion at Brackenridge. "In the course of studying the ant communities here in the 1970s," Larry recalls, "one of my Ph.D. students, Don Feener, noticed phorid flies altering the outcome of competition." Don was studying native ant species. He observed that if two species of ants were trying to get the same food and a phorid fly started bothering one ant, that ant would run away and hide, leaving the other ant to get the food. A second student of Larry's, Bill Marshall, had also seen phorid flies attacking the native species of Texas fire ant, *Solenopsis geminata*. "Because we knew the native fire ants also had phorid flies and we saw this competitive interaction," Larry says, "it was a natural thing to start thinking about using phorids against the imported fire ants."

Larry arranged to send a team to South America to see whether or not the phorids there affect fire ants in their native homes. They do. With phorids buzzing around, fire ants do not dominate other ant species as they do in the United States. Brazil, for instance, has only one-fifth the number of fire ant mounds as the southeastern United States.

To Larry, the next step was obvious.

Phorids lay their eggs inside of ants' bodies, killing them. It's the ants' reactions to the flies, however, that are even more important.

THE PHORID FACTORY

In the mid-1990s, Larry began assembling a phorid fly factory. With money from Texas ranchers, he partnered up with scientists in Brazil and then Argentina. These scientists identified at least a dozen phorid fly species from South America that attacked fire ants. Larry and his team selected two phorid species to breed and release

CLOCKWISE FROM RIGHT:

In their native Brazil and Argentina, fire ants live at much lower densities than they do in the United States. Phorid flies may be the key.

After the ants are parasitized by the flies, they are kept in little "ant hotels" until the flies hatch.

Larry Gilbert's lab keeps dozens of fire ant colonies in plastic tubs. They use these colonies to raise phorid flies and study fly-ant relationships.

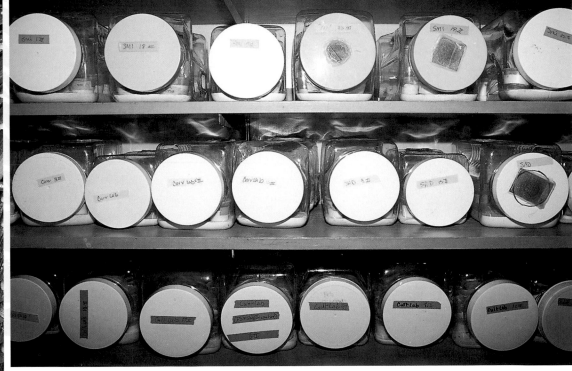

16

How Expensive Is an Ant?

Besides taking a terrible toll on native wildlife, many invasive species cost us billions of dollars in economic losses. According to a 2001 study, each year Texans spend $1.2 *billion* on controlling fire ants and repairing damage they cause. Of this, $700 million is spent by individual households. According to the United States Department of Agriculture (USDA), annual nationwide costs approach $5 billion! Of this, $3.6 billion are spent repairing and replacing fire ant damage; $1.35 billion are spent trying to control the ants; and $50 million are spent on medical treatment for fire ant stings. The ants cost farmers an additional $750 million in lost crops and damaged equipment.

Dr. Sanford Porter of the USDA in Gainesville, Florida, has played a vital role in researching and releasing phorid flies.

as biological control—or "biocontrol"—agents for the red imported fire ant (see sidebar: "Farming Phorids").

During this same time, one of Larry's first postdoctoral students, Dr. Sanford Porter, was conducting a similar program in Florida with funding from the U.S. Department of Agriculture. Both programs had successes and failures. Eventually, however, the phorids began taking hold.

In Florida, by the year 2007, the fly *Pseudacteon tricuspis* had spread through more than 33,400 square miles—an area the size of Maine. By 2006, that same fly had occupied more than 7,800 square miles of central and coastal Texas. According to studies by Ed LeBrun, these flies were expanding their ranges by five to forty-five miles per year. In Texas, many of these releases were conducted by Larry's laboratory. Others were released by Texas A&M University. A second species of phorid, *Pseudacteon curvatas*, had also become established.

And that leads to a big question: Will phorids finally break the fire ants' grip on the Southeast?

For Larry, the answer is "possibly"—but not just yet.

WANTED: A FOUNTAIN OF PHORIDS

A major drawback of the phorids currently spreading through Florida and Texas is that they mainly attack ants at mounds that have been disturbed by large animals, weather, and other events. The flies kill the ants that they parasitize, but they probably have little effect on the

LEFT: Several full-time technicians are needed to keep the phorid factory going. Here, a lab tech uses a sucking tube to remove phorids from an "attack chamber."

ABOVE: Field technicians monitor ant numbers before and after phorid flies are released.

FACING: As red imported fire ant numbers decline, it allows native ants such as this harvester ant, or "pogo," to return.

colonies as a whole. What's needed, in Larry's view, is a whole community of phorids, like the community that the fire ants face in Brazil and Argentina. What's *especially* needed are phorids that attack fire ants while they're out looking for food. By disrupting the fire ants' ability to find and harvest food supplies, the flies could have a dramatic effect on ant populations.

Larry's laboratory is in the process of releasing just such a phorid, a species called *Pseudacteon obtusus*. However, patience will still be required. Larry thinks it will take a long time to reduce fire ants to the level they are at in their native countries. "I would say it's going to be more than ten years before these flies do anything. It's the whole-community effect that may be the most important thing rather than any one magic bullet." What's new and exciting in the battle against fire ants is that now, at last, scientists have a weapon with a real chance to knock these invaders back down to size.

Farming Phorids

Introducing phorid flies into fire ant populations requires a huge effort. "You have to gradually build up the fly populations," Larry Gilbert explains. "It takes a long time."

STEP ONE: NABBING A NEST

The first step is to go out and dig up a colony of fire ants. Larry's technicians bring the ants back in buckets and then sift them by size. Why? Because phorid flies come in different sizes, and each species needs a certain size of ant to develop properly. In some phorid species, the size of the ant also determines the sex of the fly that grows in it. Smaller ants produce male flies, while larger ants produce females. To establish a breeding population of flies, a lab must make sure they turn out a good mix of females and males.

In this ant "inoculation chamber," a computer raises and lowers these shelters. This keeps ants on the move and gives phorids a better chance to inject them with their eggs.

Stacks of screens sort new ant colonies by size.

STEP TWO: ANT INJECTION

After sifting, ants are placed in different containers—called attack or inoculation chambers—where they are exposed to the phorid flies. The flies attack the ants, injecting their eggs into each ant's thorax.

STEP THREE: BAKING A FLY

After the ants are injected with fly eggs, they are placed in little plastic tubs, or "ant hotels," while the fly larvae grow inside of them. "The egg hatches," Ed LeBrun continues, "and then the first instar larva moves up through the

After the ants' heads fall off, they are placed in these chambers until the fly larvae emerge as adult flies.

An adult phorid fly emerging from the head of a fire ant.

thorax into the ant's head. As the larva grows, it feeds largely on the blood of the ant. Then the final stage of the larva starts feeding on the muscle tissues and the nervous tissues of the head, so that's what eventually kills the ant."

"If you hate fire ants," Larry Gilbert adds, "you love this."

STEP FOUR: GATHERING AND RELEASING FLIES

As the ants die, their heads fall off and the fly pupae or cocoons form inside. Larry's lab techs gather up all the ant heads. Then, as soon as the flies begin to hatch, the techs rush the flies out into the field. "Generation time is about a month from egg to adult," says Ed LeBrun. "The adult can live for about a week, so you've got to get them out into the field pretty quick."

Keeping the entire operation going is complicated and expensive. At any one time, Larry's group keeps about sixty fire ant colonies going in the lab. Sometimes a fungus or other disease wipes out one of the colonies. Overall, though, Larry's group has been able to raise and release more than 300,000 flies since the fly factory began—about one fly for every two people in Austin, Texas.

CHAPTER THREE:

Melaleuca Madness

Tropical sun pounds down on the men as they squish forward into a dense thicket of melaleuca (MEL-ah-LUKE-ah), or "paperbark," trees. Dressed only in short pants and rubber boots, each man carries a bottle of poisonous blue herbicide in one hand and in the other, a machete. Blades flashing, the men attack the melaleuca trees. Small trees fall with a single stroke. Larger trees are "girdled"—cut so that the outer growth layer, or cambium, is severed around the entire tree trunk. Once a trunk is cut down or girdled, each man sprays blue herbicide on the stump to make sure the tree will not grow back again. Then he quickly moves on to the next tree.

In a single day, the fifteen-man crew can chop down fifteen, twenty, forty acres of melaleuca. That may sound like a lot, but until recently, control efforts such as these couldn't even keep up with new areas that were being infested *every day*. Now, farmers, ranchers, and other land managers have a new tool—one that is starting to subdue one of our nation's worst invaders.

DEMON FROM DOWN UNDER

Unlike the red imported fire ant, *Melaleuca quinquenervia* was brought to the United States on purpose. Around the year 1900, people started importing it from Australia. The tree looked nice, and land developers used it to stabilize loose soils. People also thought the tree might be good for timber. Over the next forty years, it was heavily planted along canals, while airplanes dropped millions of the plants' seeds to help dry up the "worthless swamp" known as the Everglades.

But melaleuca didn't exactly follow the game plan. It turned out to be useless for timber, and the tree quickly began invading new areas all on its own. By the 1990s, this harmless-looking plant had infested about one-fifth of South Florida's total land area.

The tree from Down Under had become a nightmare.

TURNING WONDERS INTO WASTELANDS

The Everglades is one of our nation's richest and most spectacular natural wonders. This giant "river of grass" attracts millions of tourists. It protects water supplies and provides homes for hundreds of different plant and animal species. Melaleuca, though, turns Everglades ecosystems into biological wastelands. The trees form impenetrable thickets of up to 45,000 trees *per acre*. That is like having *one thousand trees* growing in your school classroom!

In such densities, other plants and animals don't have a chance. A

FACING: Even experienced crews cannot keep up with new melaleuca infestations.

pristine Everglades wetlands may have sixty to eighty species of plants living in an area, but once melaleuca moves in, that number can drop to three or four. Native animals fare no better, since melaleuca provides almost no useable food or habitat.

Just as alarming, melaleuca forests are extremely flammable. Every year, huge, dangerous wildfires roar through South Florida's melaleuca forests. The trees' thick, papery bark and the oils in their leaves provide the perfect fuel for raging conflagrations. To top it off, about 20 percent of humans are allergic to melaleuca pollen.

By the 1980s, the melaleuca problem had become so bad that Florida's land managers were in despair. They could poison the tree and cut it down, but any gains they made were soon undone. New melaleuca seedlings were infesting up to fifty acres of new territory *every day*, and nothing seemed to stop them. Land managers and scientists decided it was time to get serious.

TEAMWORK

Dr. Ted Center directs the Invasive Plant Research Laboratory, a facility run by the U.S. Department of Agriculture in Fort Lauderdale, Florida. He has battled invasive species since he was a university student in the 1970s. Ted remembers how he and his colleagues first started fighting back against melaleuca. "Nobody put us together," he recalls. "We all kind of drifted together and we started this group called

Everglades Magic

The Everglades environment is unlike any other found on our planet. Fed by a fifty-mile-wide, slow-moving river that flows from Lake Okeechobee to the tip of Florida, the Everglades give rise to a smorgasbord of habitats from freshwater meadows to "hammocks" of hardwood trees. These places provide homes for at least fifteen endangered species, including the Florida panther, American crocodile, red-cockaded woodpecker, and manatee. The Everglades offer key feeding and resting areas for thousands of wading birds every year. However, human development—including the draining of large parts of South Florida—has severely damaged the Everglades environment. Current efforts hope to restore water flows through the Everglades and return this special place to some of its former glory.

the Exotic Pest Plant Council. Most of the people who were there were people who just didn't know what to do about melaleuca. So people started getting together and comparing notes."

Ted and his team became especially interested in how biological control agents might be used to get a handle on melaleuca. In its native Australia, melaleuca is uncommon. In some areas, it's even considered a threatened species. Ted suspected that the reason for this is that melaleuca has natural enemies in Australia that knock it back—enemies that are not present in the United States.

"We had a laboratory in Queensland, Australia, that was part of our own laboratory," Ted explains, "and we got a little bit of money from the U.S. Army Corps of Engineers to do preliminary surveys of insects in Australia." After three years, Ted's Australian teammates had compiled a list of more than 450 species of insects that attacked melaleuca. Was it possible that some of these could help beat back the tree in the United States? Ted thought so.

BIOLOGY BUSTERS

"Before we even started the surveys," Ted recalls, "I reviewed the biology of melaleuca and tried to figure out what we needed to do to the tree to combat it. As I read about it, I realized that the flowers are produced by the tips of the shoots, or branches, and as the shoots grow, they keep producing flowers. So I thought, 'That may be the weak point.'"

Melaleuca flowers and the seedpods they produce, in fact, are a big part of what makes the plant such a fearsome invader. A single melaleuca tree can store up to 100 *million* seeds at a time. When the tree is burned, cut down, or stressed in other ways, its seedpods burst

LEFT: Melaleuca flowers grow at the tips of the branches. MIDDLE: When the tree is stressed, a melaleuca's seedpods can release millions of seeds. RIGHT: Tiny melaleuca seeds are easily carried by the wind—one reason the tree spreads so rapidly.

open and wind transports the tiny seeds for miles. Ted and his colleagues reasoned that if they could find an insect or disease that attacked the tips of the tree branches, that might halt the tree's reproduction. After searching high and low, their Australian teammates came up with an insect that might just do the trick. It was a little beetle called *Oxyops vitiosa*, the melaleuca leaf weevil.

CHOW TIME

The melaleuca weevil appeared to do exactly what scientists wanted. Its larvae chewed up the leaves at the very ends of melaleuca branches, preventing flowers from growing. Finding the weevil, however, was just the beginning. Like Larry Gilbert's team in Texas, Ted Center's team had to make sure the weevil would not harm any desirable species. They went through something called "host-specificity testing"—testing the weevil on dozens of different plants to make sure it fed only on melaleuca. Then they had to get a permit from the USDA to release the weevil into the field.

It was a painfully long process.

"We first got the weevil into quarantine in Florida in 1992," Ted recalls. "The host-specificity testing was not finished until 1996. And we didn't get the permit to release it until 1997."

Once they had their permit, however, Ted and his team rushed the weevil out to a melaleuca-infested wetlands near Fort Lauderdale. The scientists anxiously wondered if the weevil would survive Florida's climate, let alone spread through the melaleuca forests. "They weren't reproducing very much when we first released them, which had us worried," Ted remembers. "Then October came around and the plants started growing all these buds and producing new foliage, and the weevils took off."

Still, the weevils had drawbacks. They spread very slowly—only about half a mile per year. Also, when the weevil larvae pupated, they dropped to the soil before emerging as adults. "So if the soil is flooded," explains Ted's colleague Cressida Silvers, "they're going to drown. If an area is

How Many Agencies Does It Take to Kill a Tree?

To fund its efforts, the melaleuca biological control program has depended on many different agencies. These include the U.S. Army Corps of Engineers, the South Florida Water Management District, the University of Florida, the Florida Department of Environmental Protection, the Departments of Environmental Resource Management in Broward and Miami-Dade Counties, and Australia's Commonwealth Scientific and Industrial Research Organization. The involvement of so many organizations reveals how important it is to rid Florida of this pervasive pest.

permanently flooded or flooded for most of the year, those populations are not going to build up."

As the weevil populations were slowly spreading through Florida, however, a new insect arrived on the scene—the melaleuca psyllid (SIL-id), *Boreioglycaspis melaleucae*.

REINFORCEMENTS

Ted's colleagues discovered the psyllid in one of their greenhouses in Australia. Unlike the weevil, which was a chewing insect, the psyllid was a sucking insect. It pierced the tissues of melaleuca leaves and sucked the juices out of them. Best of all, both the weevil and the psyllid

attacked the tips of melaleuca branches. Again, it was the larvae and not the adult insects that did most of the damage. Ted and his colleagues hoped that working together, the weevil and psyllid might accomplish more than either one alone.

They began testing the psyllid in 1998 and first released it in 2002. What happened next exceeded the scientists' wildest dreams. By 2002, the weevil was chewing its way through many different areas of South Florida. When the psyllid was released, however, it spread much more quickly. Together, the two insects became a formidable match for melaleuca.

TAMEING MELALEUCA

"The biocontrol impacts really have been most dramatic in the last three or four years," Paul Pratt explains. Paul is one of Ted Center's colleagues and the director of the TAME project. TAME stands for The Area-wide Management and Evaluation of *Melaleuca quinquernervia*. It is a $5 million, five-year project to help spread biocontrol agents and educate people about managing melaleuca. Paul Pratt appreciates what a vital role the weevil and psyllid have played in melaleuca control.

"Ranchers, farmers, and other land managers treat their melaleuca as quickly and effectively as they possibly can according to the funds they have," Paul explains. "But they have neighbors on all four sides. Some of those neighbors don't have the inclination or money to spray or cut down their melaleuca plants. So as desperate as a land manager may be to get rid of his own melaleuca, he's still at the mercy of his neighbors to treat *their* plants so that new seeds won't get onto his property.

"What biocontrol brings to land managers," Paul says, "is that the insects don't recognize boundaries or fence lines. They feed throughout the region and keep the reproduction of the plant in check. So as land managers are clearing their melaleuca, they don't have to worry about their neighbors' seeds."

But the weevil and psyllid are also helping in other ways. By feeding

ABOVE: TAME project coordinator Cressida Silvers shows the enclosures where the melaleuca leaf weevil and psyllids are raised for release.

FACING: The melaleuca leaf weevil attacked the tree where it hurt most—at its flowers.

mostly on new growth, they keep melaleuca from growing back nearly as fast after it's been cut down. This means land doesn't have to be treated as often as it did before. The insects are also killing new trees. In one study, feeding by the psyllid alone killed 65 percent of melaleuca seedlings. In another study, the two insects together killed 83 percent of young melaleuca trees.

Even more dramatic, the insects are taking the fight into the heart of untreated melaleuca forests.

LEFT: Adult psyllids, shown mating, spread rapidly, increasing the damage their larvae do to melaleuca trees.

RIGHT: Like the leaf weevil, the larva of the melaleuca psyllid attacks the plant's new growth, cutting down flower and seed production.

ABOVE: Dr. Paul Pratt directs TAME—a five-year project to promote biological control and other methods for knocking back melaleuca.

RIGHT: Even if a landowner controls his melaleuca, a neighbor might not. Biocontrol agents, however, limit the seeds a neighbor's trees spread.

UNRAVELING THE INVASIVE FOREST

Dr. Min Rayamajhi has been keeping track of how the biological control agents have affected melaleuca forests. Between 1997 and 2005, Min and his colleagues studied three melaleuca locations. They monitored the numbers of trees at each site, their sizes, and the impacts of the weevil and psyllid. What they found was that the insects—along with a new disease called *Puccinia psidii*, or guava rust—have significantly reduced the overall cover of melaleuca trees in their study areas.

"When we were working ten years ago," he recalls, "we could not walk straight because of the tree density. We could hardly see, it was so dark. Now, at one site, we have about eighty-five

Counting the Costs of Melaleuca

As expensive as it is to develop biological control agents to control melaleuca, it's a bargain compared to other methods. Mechanically removing an acre of melaleuca costs $842 per acre, while injecting an acre of trees with herbicides costs $538. Federal, state, and county agencies have already spent $35 million on control programs. To treat the entire area infesting South Florida a single time would cost $421 million by mechanical removal or $269 million using herbicides. Herbicides have the added disadvantage of poisoning water supplies and harming other plant and animal species.

Treatment costs aren't the only bills melaleuca racks up, however. Economic studies have shown that failure to control melaleuca would result in more than $168 million each year in lost revenues from tourism to the Florida Everglades. Any way you add it, melaleuca has been a costly invader.

percent density reduction and the tree crowns have thinned because all these leaves have come down."

By steadily sapping the plants' reserves, the insects are even killing adult sixty- and seventy-foot-tall trees. As the melaleuca trees begin to die, native plants are beginning to return. At one of Min's sites, the number of plant species increased from ten to twenty-seven between 1997 and 2006. As the plants return, animals return, too. "Ten years ago," Min says, "the biodiversity was just not there. The forest was dominated by one thing, melaleuca. Now you go into the same place and the melaleuca is declining and it's much more natural. The melaleuca is behaving. It's not aggressive anymore."

Will insects and disease reduce melaleuca to the same extent that it exists in Australia?

"Yeah. I think so," Ted Center ventures. "We're seeing it already. Maybe even below what it is in Australia. And you don't have to kill every tree. You can sterilize it with the insects. Sterilized, a melaleuca tree is no longer a problem. Land managers can go in and remove it whenever they get around to it. So that's what we're seeing now. The trees are just not producing the high number of seeds, and the management agencies can take their dear, sweet time to clear the areas that are infested."

LEFT: Research by Dr. Min Rayamajhi has shown that biological control agents are doing major damage to melaleuca forests and helping to restore natural ecosystems.

FACING: Thanks to melaleuca-eating insects, this wetland has a good chance of staying melaleuca-free.

CHAPTER FOUR

Our Best Defenses

Using biological control agents, scientists have moved closer to achieving victory over both red imported fire ants and melaleuca—two of our worst invaders. Unfortunately, thousands of destructive invasive species are still rampaging across our country and neither the money nor the know-how is available to tackle them. Because of this, it's far cheaper—and smarter—to keep species from getting here in the first place than to try to get rid of them after they've arrived.

Mike Pitzler is the state director for the USDA's Animal and Plant Health Inspection Service in Hawaii and Guam. He is in charge of fifty employees and a $4 million annual budget devoted exclusively to the brown tree snake. About a million of those dollars are used to restore and protect Guam's native birds and bats, as well as reduce the number of power outages the snakes cause. The Guam team, for instance, has set up intensive snake control to keep snakes out of a 1,500-acre forest that protects endangered Mariana crows. In the past eight years, it has also captured and poisoned more than seven thousand snakes near fifteen power stations on the island. The rest of that money,

LEFT: The brown tree snake and other invasive species would have a huge impact on Hawaii's tourist industry.

RIGHT: A dog's sense of smell makes the animal a crucial weapon in finding brown tree snakes in cargo areas.

FACING: Live-bait traps and fence patrols keep the vast majority of brown tree snakes from crossing the fence lines into Guam's ports. Prevention is the name of the game in keeping the brown tree snake out of Hawaii and other Pacific islands.

however, is used to keep the brown tree snake out of Hawaii and other Pacific islands. Mike has no doubt that his agency's efforts are worth it.

"The brown tree snake is a major threat," Mike says. "It's safe to say that if the snake got to Hawaii it would have a major economic impact because of the tourism industry here. I think three hundred million is probably a low estimate of the damage it would cost in lost tourism to our state. That's three hundred million dollars a *year*.

"Ecologically," Mike adds, "it would be extremely disastrous as well. Already, Hawaii is number one of all the states that are impacted by invasive species. This would be another monster." Mike believes that Hawaii's bird life, like Guam's, would be especially vulnerable. About half of Hawaii's forty honeycreeper species have already gone extinct because of habitat loss, introduced diseases, and other invasive species. The brown tree snake could easily be the final death knell for the rest of these spectacular, brightly colored birds.

BROWN TREE SNAKE BATTLE STATIONS

With so much riding on prevention, the USDA does everything it can to keep the snakes from getting off Guam. Guam has five ports of exit

for military and commercial transportation. "The idea," explains operations chief Dan Vice, "is we do population control of brown tree snakes around the ports of exit by trapping the snakes and catching them by hand. These activities reduce the number of snakes that get into actual cargo areas."

Each year, USDA agents catch about six thousand brown tree snakes along Guam's port perimeters. Two-thirds are caught in traps that use live and dead mice as bait. One-third are caught by hand during regular nighttime patrols of the fence lines. About fifteen snakes a year, however, get into the cargo areas. And that's where the dog teams come in.

"The dog," Dan Vice explains, "is much better at detecting the snakes than a person. A human being can look for snakes and visually inspect things for snakes, but you don't have the ability to see things in dark spaces." With their extraordinary sense of smell, on the other hand, dogs can detect snakes even inside of crates and vehicles.

But are USDA agents catching every last snake?

"The snakes can and still do get off-island," Dan admits. "As recently as about a year and a half ago, a live snake hid in a shipment of ammunition and made it to Oklahoma." But so far, the program has kept Hawaii safe. "In the ten years before our program became operational in 1993," Mike Pitzler explains, "there were seven brown tree snake captures on Oahu. Seven live brown tree snakes that made it to Hawaii. There was one in 1994, the year after. Since that time, there's been zero."

These numbers make it clear that active prevention efforts such as the brown tree snake program are a sound investment. Another is education.

A MUSSEL MUSCLES IN

Doug Jensen works for the University of Minnesota Sea Grant, part of a partnership between the federal government and the state of Minnesota to study, protect, and improve the state's aquatic environments. A tall, strapping figure, Doug has a friendly personality that is well suited to his job—to educate the public about aquatic invasive species that threaten Minnesota's lakes and rivers. Sitting at the top of his "hit list" is a small shelled animal called the zebra mussel.

The zebra mussel, *Dreissena polymorpha*, reached the Great Lakes in the mid-1980s. Larvae of the mussel were probably transported to the lakes in the ballast water of commercial ships from Europe. Ballast water helps stabilize ships, especially those that are not fully loaded. Usually, the water is pumped into a ship at one

CLOCKWISE FROM TOP:

For Doug Jensen, educating people about invasive species is the key to keeping Minnesota's remaining lakes healthy and pest-free.

Using his homemade mussel catcher, Doug scrapes pilings in Duluth Harbor for zebra mussels.

Despite Lake Superior's cold temperatures, zebra mussels have totally colonized the habitat of Duluth Harbor.

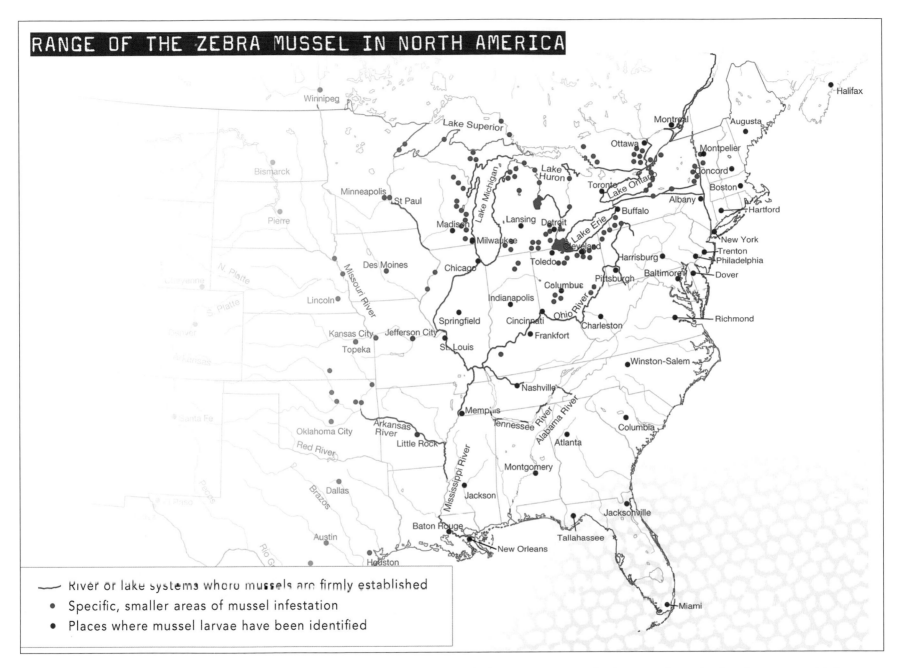

RANGE OF THE ZEBRA MUSSEL IN NORTH AMERICA

— River or lake systems where mussels are firmly established
• Specific, smaller areas of mussel infestation
• Places where mussel larvae have been identified

Since it was first detected in the mid-1980s, the zebra mussel has invaded many of our nation's most important waterways and lakes.

Getting Tough on Ballast Water

As harmful as the zebra mussel has been, it is only one of thousands of species that have been transported in ballast water. At some time in their lives, most aquatic animals exist as tiny larval stages that can be sucked into—and dumped out of—a ship's ballast tanks. According to the West Coast Ballast Outreach Project, "It is estimated that on any one day more than five thousand species of freshwater, brackish, and marine organisms may be transported in ballast water in ocean-going vessels around the world." The problem threatens aquatic environments worldwide. More than 250 introduced species have invaded San Francisco Bay, for example, all but wiping out native species. In the Great Lakes, at least 183 non-native species have been introduced, many through ballast water discharge.

The magnitude of the ballast water problem has spurred countries around the world to cooperate on solving it. Many invaders can be eliminated simply by exchanging ballast water far offshore. Industry is also looking for ways to kill organisms in ballast water using chemicals, electricity, and other methods. The United States and California, Oregon, Washington, and Michigan have passed laws to deal with ballast water. Many countries are also pushing for international laws. Extensive damage has been done to aquatic ecosystems already, but new laws and enforcement offer hope that invasions will decrease in the future.

Ballast water from cargo ships helps transport not only zebra mussels but hundreds of aquatic invasive species around the world.

port and discharged at another. In the process, this water carries a host of unwanted organisms, including the larvae of zebra mussels.

Zebra mussels grow to only a couple of inches long, but few invasive species have caused so much damage in such a short amount of time. "Zebra mussels are a huge problem," Doug Jensen explains. "Except for the sea lamprey, they've been one of the Great Lakes' most important invasive species, because they affect everyone."

How bad are they?

In some places, the mussels grow at densities of up to 700,000 per square yard—a number almost impossible to imagine. The mussels grow so thickly that they block intakes for drinking water, nuclear power plants, hospitals, and irrigation systems. They clog boat engines and hulls. They can eliminate up to 98 percent of native clams and other shellfish populations by suffocating them and preventing them from feeding and moving. Many scientists also believe that by gobbling up food for other animals, the mussels are driving important Great Lakes fisheries to collapse.

But even after the mussels spread through all of the Great Lakes and into the Mississippi River basin, not everyone was ready to declare defeat in the zebra mussel conflict.

ZEROING IN ON ZEBRA MUSSELS

While people throughout the Midwest looked on in horror as the zebra mussel took over their waterways, Minnesotans realized something important: even though the zebra mussel was in the Great Lakes, Minnesota still had 15,000 other lakes to protect. Instead of just waiting for the zebra mussel to spread, they had an opportunity to head it off at the pass.

"In the early 1990s," Doug explains, "Minnesota got tough on aquatic invasive species. The state authorized its Department of Natural Resources to develop a prevention program based on education, watercraft inspection, monitoring, and enforcement."

Boaters are a key to the spread of zebra mussels, because the mussels attach to boat hulls and motors. Even worse, adult mussels can survive up to three weeks out of the water. So if boaters are moving between different lakes, they can easily transport zebra mussels with them. To reach boaters, the state performs boat inspections, erects signs, runs ads, and performs many other prevention activities. One burning question Doug Jensen had, however, was "How effective was Minnesota's zebra mussel program compared to other states'?"

Doug conducted surveys of boaters in five states. He especially wanted to know If boaters were concerned enough to take action to prevent zebra mussels from spreading. "What we found in our survey is that more than ninety percent of boaters in Minnesota are taking action to prevent the spread of zebra mussels." In states that did not have effective education programs, as few as 30 percent of boaters were taking action. The impacts of education have been clearly felt. In Minnesota, zebra mussels have spread to only four other lakes since the 1990s. In nearby Michigan, by 2006, the mussels had invaded 233 other lakes— with devastating consequences.

ABOVE: Minnesota's public education campaign proves that it pays to prevent invasive species before they spread.

LEFT: Boaters and other water sports enthusiasts can easily spread invasive species without knowing it. A new campaign to address this problem nationwide is "Stop Aquatic Hitchhikers!" A project of the Aquatic Nuisance Species Task Force, the U.S. Fish and Wildlife Service, and the U.S. Coast Guard, the program aims to educate water enthusiasts in how to protect the waters that they love.

NATIONAL LESSONS

Minnesota's successful programs have been used to develop nationwide guidelines to stop the spread of zebra mussels and other aquatic invasive species. Unfortunately, efforts to halt invasive species suffer from two serious problems.

ABOVE: In the United States, poor government funding limits scientific research on invasive species—and our ability to keep them from spreading.

LEFT AND FACING: New Zealand's tough invasive species laws should be a model for all countries for how to control these harmful organisms and help protect animals such as the endangered tuatara (AT LEFT).

Those that are have only enough staff and resources to work on a handful of species. Funding shortages also hamper public education, watercraft inspections, and other key prevention efforts.

A second, serious problem is the way we deal with invasive species. Instead of working to keep invasive species from reaching our shores, we tend to wait until they are already here. APHIS—the USDA's Animal and Plant Health Inspection Service—does a fair job inspecting for diseases and pests *on* plants and animals imported into the United States. They rarely, however, evaluate the plants and animals themselves to see if they might *become* pests. Our laws still allow most plants and animals to be imported into the United States until they are proven to be a problem. A much smarter approach would be to keep out plants and animals until they are proven to be *safe*.

The country of New Zealand has taken just such an approach. In 1996, it passed laws requiring that any new organism brought into the country be fully evaluated to see if it poses a threat to New Zealand's environment, economy, or public health. Only organisms that are proved safe can be imported. Following New Zealand's example would help all nations—including the United States—greatly reduce the cost and suffering caused by the spread of invasive organisms. As Minnesota's zebra mussel program has demonstrated, however, personal responsibility plays a key role in stopping invasive species.

"Funding always is the number one limiting factor," says Ted Center. Invasive species cost the United States about $137 *billion* every year. Yet in 2006, for example, the federal government budgeted only $4 million for scientific research on aquatic invasive species *nationwide* —a little more than a penny for every man, woman, and child. The result is that there are not nearly enough labs working on invasive species.

HUMAN BEINGS: THE KEY INVADER

Human beings are without a doubt the most important invasive species on the planet. Not only have we colonized every corner of the earth, but we are responsible for the spread of almost all other invasive species.

Unlike other invasive species, however, we can change our behaviors to improve the situation. Below are guidelines you can—and should—follow to prevent the spread of invasive species. By doing so, you are making a real difference in keeping our world a safer, healthier, more enjoyable place to live.

A GUIDE TO STOPPING INVASIVE SPECIES

• **Never, ever release fish, reptiles, or other exotic organisms into the wild.** Many invasive species were originally pets or plants that people grew tired of and released. Remember: when you buy a pet, it is your responsibility for the rest of *the pet's* lifetime. If you aren't prepared to care for a pet or plant until its death, don't get one.

• **Never release or dump aquarium plants where they might reach open waterways.** Aquarium plants pose an especially dangerous threat to natural ecosystems. Never allow pieces of plants or seeds to go down drains. If you are disposing of the plants, treat them with bleach until you are sure they are dead before putting them in the garbage.

• **Make sure your cats and dogs are neutered or spayed** so they won't produce unwanted offspring that prey on native birds and other wildlife.

• **Urge your parents and friends to plant only native species in yards and gardens.** This reduces the chances that an exotic plant will escape to become invasive. Native plants are also often easier to take care of and provide better food and shelter to native animals.

• **Never carry live plants or animals with you when you travel.** Also, never carry products that are made from living organisms unless they have been certified "pest-free."

Dude, Get Some Habitattitude™

Habitattitude™
PROTECT OUR ENVIRONMENT
DO NOT RELEASE FISH AND AQUATIC PLANTS

www.Habitattitude.net

Some of our worst invasive species have been released by aquarium and pet owners. When these owners have grown tired of their animals, they've simply released them into the environment—sometimes with devastating results. To keep this from happening in the future, government agencies teamed up with the pet industry to create the Habitattitude™ campaign. The campaign's goals are to make pet and aquarium owners, pond owners, and water gardeners aware of the problem of aquatic invasive species and to provide guidelines for safely disposing of unwanted aquatic animals and plants. To learn more about the program, log on to the Habitattitude™ website, www.habitattitude.net.

Never, <u>ever</u> release pets, aquarium fish, or aquarium plants into the wild. By properly disposing of these organisms, you may prevent a disaster.

• **Scrub the soles of your shoes before you travel to other places or go hiking in natural areas.** Also scrub them when you return. Many seeds and eggs of exotic species are too small for us to notice but travel quite well on the bottoms of shoes.

• **If you are a boater, inspect and remove aquatic plants, animals, and mud from your boat, motor, and trailer**. Drain water from watercraft. Rinse everything with high-pressure hot water, or dry everything for at least five days. Also dispose of unwanted live bait and worms in the trash.

• **Control invasive species on your property or in your community.** Volunteer in community "weed out" days or invasive species weeks or months.

• **Always fill out a declaration card when you are traveling across international borders.** List all fruits, vegetables, and other prohibited items you are carrying.

• **Write to your members of Congress, your senators, and other political representatives.** Urge them to pass stricter regulations on importing exotic species and releasing genetically engineered organisms. Also, tell them to provide more resources to prevent, control, and minimize the impacts of invasive species.

• **Educate your friends and family about invasive species and the threats they pose to all of us.**

Butterfly gardens are a great way to encourage native plants and the native animals that use them.

GLOSSARY

alien: originating somewhere else (see **exotic**).

ballast: water, rocks, or other heavy materials placed in the bottom hold of a ship to help stabilize it in the water.

biocontrol: a means of using living organisms to control pests.

biodiversity: the total variety or sum of species living in an area; also the variety or sum of ecosystems and genetic diversity.

biological control agent or biocontrol agent: a living organism that attacks, kills, or controls a pest.

competitive interaction: any interaction between two different species of organisms that use the same resource.

ecosystem: a community of organisms along with the physical space it occupies.

established species: a species that is able to survive and reproduce in a place or situation.

exotic species: a living species originating from somewhere else.

host-specificity testing: the process of determining if a potential biocontrol agent will attack only its intended target.

instar: a developmental stage in the growth of an insect or other arthropod larva; after each instar, the larva sheds its shell or outer skin, allowing it to grow bigger until it becomes an adult.

invasive species: an exotic, or alien, species that causes problems in its new environment.

land manager: a person responsible for taking care of a large piece of land. Land managers can include farmers, ranchers, wildlife and parks biologists —even water district personnel.

larvae: the early life stages of insects and certain other organisms.

legislation: laws.

monogyne: having only one queen.

ornamental plants: plants used only for decoration or landscaping.

parasitize: to live in or on another organism while drawing nutrients directly from the body of that organism.

phorids: a group of tiny flies that parasitize ants.

polygyne: having multiple queens.

postdoctoral colleague or student: a person who has finished his or her Ph.D. but is working under the supervision of a more experienced researcher.

psyllid: one kind of insect that sucks juices from plants.

quarantine: placing a living thing in isolation until it is proven to pose no hazard to the health or well-being of others or the environment.

stand: a grove of trees.

USDA: United States Department of Agriculture.

virus: tiny parasitic organisms that live and reproduce in other organisms, usually causing disease.

weevil: a certain kind of beetle that resembles a little rhinoceros.

Zebra mussels on a boat propeller.